About This Issue Guide

THIS DISCUSSION GUIDE IS DESIGNED TO HELP AMERICANS DELIBERATE TOGETHER about what we should do to address unprecedented challenges that may hinder future generations from leading successful and economically secure lives. The guide outlines three different ways of considering the issue. Each suggests actions we might take, along with trade-offs we would have to accept. Altogether, these options allow participants to explore important values and tensions shared by many. Information in this guide raises crucial questions for which there are no easy answers.

- Will the next generation, like those before it, be able to build an economically secure future, or will it face too many unprecedented challenges that undercut its prospects?
- Should present-day priorities be more important than our obligations to future generations?
- Is the next generation receiving the education and support it needs to succeed?
- Are there disparities that we should be addressing today to enable future generations to prosper tomorrow?

Bolstering the chances of success for future generations requires us to consider choices that cut across conventional partisan lines and generational differences. What course of action should be a priority as we plan for the future?

The research conducted in developing this guide included a review of policy ideas and polling data from across the political spectrum, interviews and conversations with Americans from all walks of life, focus groups with young people, and appraisals of initial drafts by experts with diverse views and experiences.

Youth and Opportunity

What Should We Do for Future Generations to Thrive?

MANY YOUNG PEOPLE think the United States is on the wrong track and fear that decisions by today's leaders are robbing them, and those who come after them, of a better future. Distrust in political parties combined with concerns about racial inequality and the lack of fundamental fairness in our society are inspiring protests—many led by children and young adults—and fueling grassroots efforts to challenge the status quo.

Several trends threaten the health and economic prosperity of future generations:

- Young adults, earning less income and saddled by student loan debt, are not doing as well socially or economically as their parents were at the same age.

- The planet and all its inhabitants face critical danger in coming decades unless the US and every other nation grapples with the causes and effects of climate change.
- Long-standing economic and social obstacles have for too long denied opportunities to women and to millions of Americans from diverse racial and ethnic backgrounds.
- Our rising national debt will force the government to spend increasingly more of its budget paying off interest costs, leaving fewer resources to invest in future economic growth.
- The COVID-19 pandemic is limiting job prospects and leading to the ruin of many businesses, both small and large.

While young Americans want to inherit a stable economy, a cleaner environment, and a more equitable society, they worry that these are not priorities for today's policymakers.

This country, at its best, created conditions under which each generation left a stronger nation for the next. But today, for the first time in 60 years, Americans aged 35 and younger have less optimism than those aged 55 and older. Millennials and Generation Z are less satisfied with their lives, their economic outlook, their jobs, and government and business leaders, according to recent

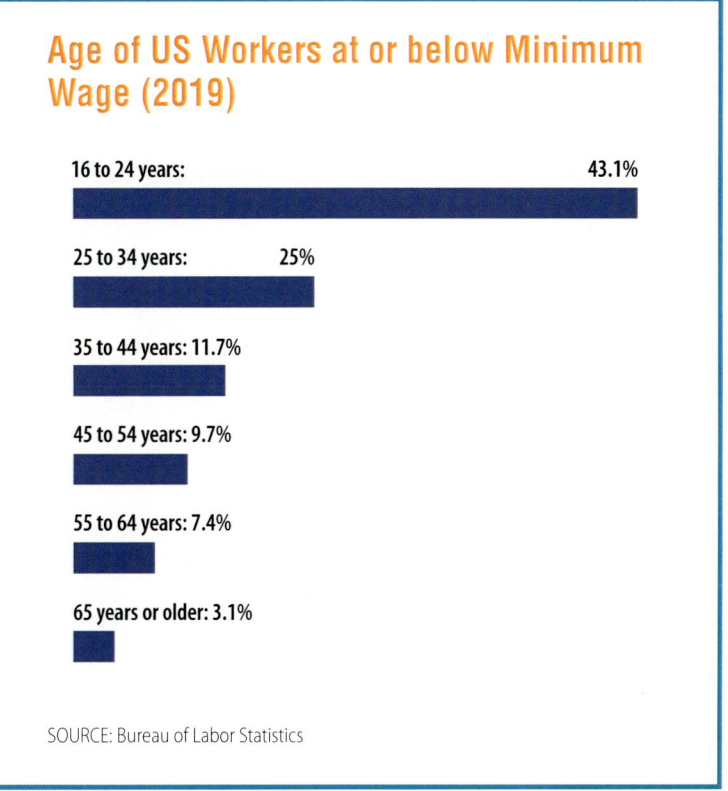

Age of US Workers at or below Minimum Wage (2019)

16 to 24 years: 43.1%

25 to 34 years: 25%

35 to 44 years: 11.7%

45 to 54 years: 9.7%

55 to 64 years: 7.4%

65 years or older: 3.1%

SOURCE: Bureau of Labor Statistics

studies by the University of Michigan and the Deloitte consulting firm.

Compared with previous generations, Millennials are less likely to own their own homes and they are more likely to be living with their parents for longer stretches of time. Millennials also hold more student loan debt than any previous generation.

Too many Americans are earning less money than their parents did. Despite being better educated, Millennials are

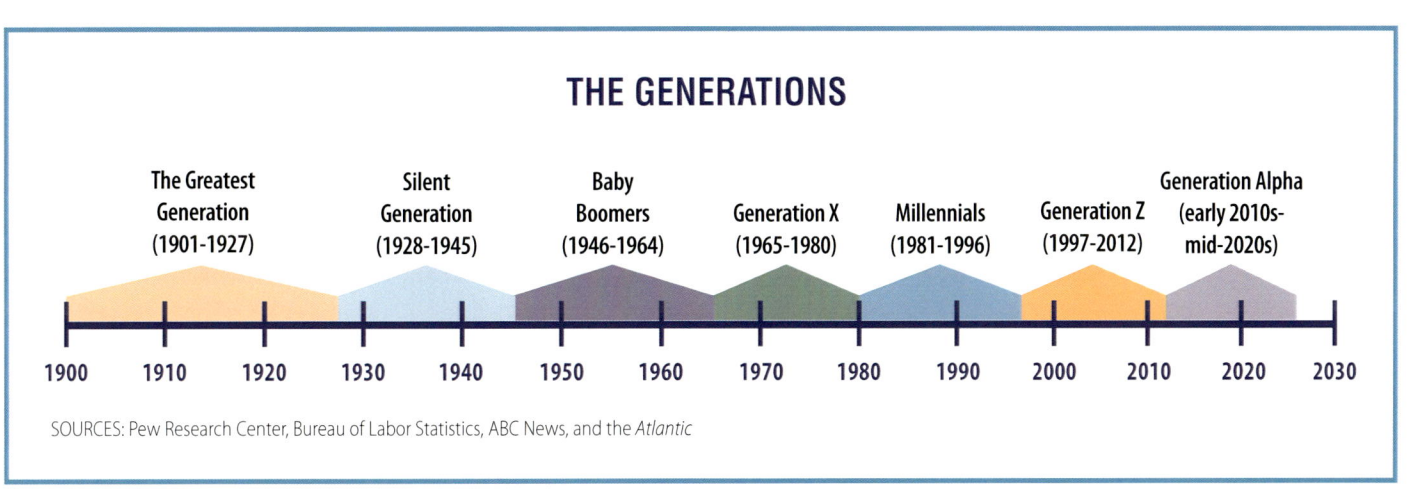

THE GENERATIONS

The Greatest Generation (1901-1927)

Silent Generation (1928-1945)

Baby Boomers (1946-1964)

Generation X (1965-1980)

Millennials (1981-1996)

Generation Z (1997-2012)

Generation Alpha (early 2010s-mid-2020s)

1900 1910 1920 1930 1940 1950 1960 1970 1980 1990 2000 2010 2020 2030

SOURCES: Pew Research Center, Bureau of Labor Statistics, ABC News, and the *Atlantic*

Jason Redmond/AFP/Getty Images

earning 20 percent less than Baby Boomers at the same stage of life, according to a 2019 analysis by New America, a public policy think tank.

Although the United States is the world's largest economy, one in six American children lives in poverty, making them the poorest age group in the country. And that poverty is not equally distributed. According to a 2020 report by the Children's Defense Fund, 73 percent of poor US children come from non-White backgrounds.

Despite these challenges, young people are taking steps to ensure that the American Dream endures. Young Americans want to improve their communities, address systemic disparities, and have an economically secure future. They are ready for change and are as willing, if not more so, than their elders to find practical solutions to difficult problems.

What Should We Do for Future Generations to Thrive?

This issue guide presents three options for creating a better future and stable economy for all young Americans.

While the options are not mutually exclusive, they do represent different ways of thinking about the problem. All options offer advantages, along with risks and trade-offs. The guide does not include every idea or strategy to address these complex and interconnected challenges, but the basic questions in this guide can help users think through various proposals and perspectives.

Option **1:**
Equip People to Succeed

THE UNITED STATES is not adequately preparing the members of the next generation for the challenges ahead, failing to ensure that they have the necessary skills to succeed in a rapidly changing world.

Compared to students from other developed countries, American students perform only slightly above average in reading and fall well behind peers in international tests of other subjects. For example, US students rank 30th in math and 19th in science, compared to students in other developed nations, according to a 2019 study by *U.S. News & World Report*. The COVID-19 coronavirus pandemic has only exacerbated problems for Millennials, Generation Z, and Generation Alpha students who do not have computers or reliable internet access to aid completion of schoolwork via remote learning. Moreover, the economic impact of COVID-19 means that many of the financial resources that help young people enter the workforce and succeed at their new jobs are being cut.

"Helping young people prepare to engage in work and life as productive adults is a central task for any society," said Martha Ross, a senior fellow at the Brookings Institution. "But after the great K-12 conveyor belt of education ends in the United States, young people out of high school face a landscape of college and training options that can be confusing, difficult to navigate, and financially out of reach—and they also face a labor market that favors those with college degrees."

Crippling student loan debt and a shortage of good mentorship and internship programs have created a gap in the critical transition from school to the workplace. The share of teens and young adults who are employed has declined steadily since about 2000, and that trend only worsened as a result of the Great Recession between 2007 and 2009 and the COVID-19 pandemic of 2020.

Entering the job market is extremely difficult for recent high school and college graduates. In the nation's largest cities and counties, 17 percent of all 18-to-24-year-olds, or 2.3 million people, were out of work in 2019, Brookings found. The number of jobless young Americans more than doubled at the onset of the pandemic.

Moreover, the pandemic highlighted the fact that many young people have mental health issues that are not being addressed. Between 40 and 50 percent of all young adults ages 18-29 reported symptoms of anxiety or depression in weekly surveys conducted in the spring and summer of 2020 by the National Center for Health Statistics and the U.S. Census Bureau. The results, not surprising in an ongoing pandemic,

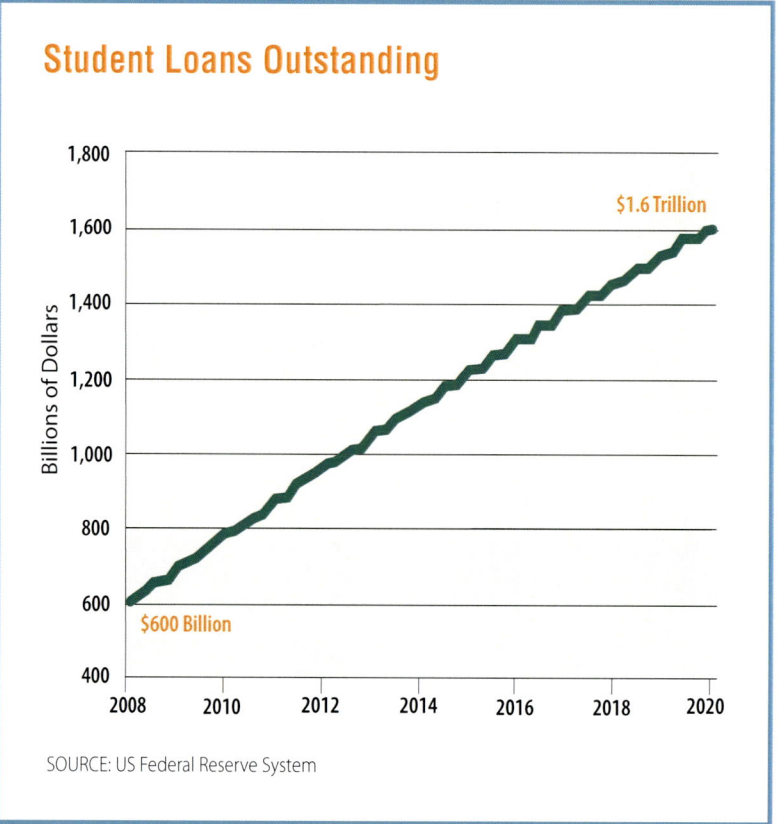

Student Loans Outstanding

SOURCE: US Federal Reserve System

nonetheless reflect a deepening of existing trends: rising anxiety, depression, and stress among young adults.

This option says future generations will have a better chance of doing well when they get the education, training, and support they need to succeed.

A Primary Drawback of This Option:
This option does too little to teach self-reliance, personal responsibility, and a good work ethic. It assumes that all challenges can be overcome with more services. But preparation doesn't always ensure success in life. Many forces determine our individual and collective futures.

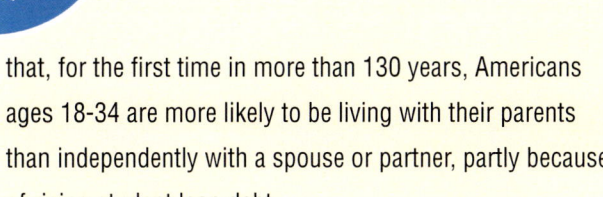

What We Should Do

Boost K-12 student achievement by reducing class sizes and providing extra support to students who need it.

Decades of research in various school districts suggests students in classrooms with 15 or fewer children achieve higher test scores and exhibit better behavior than do their peers in larger classes. A 2014 analysis by the National Education Policy Center found that the benefits of smaller classes, particularly for students from disadvantaged backgrounds, are often realized when the class is taught by skilled teachers who offer one-on-one tutoring for the students who need it.

Smaller classes were found to have the greatest positive effect on young learners who were inattentive or withdrawn. "In a big class, everybody in the back of the room is talking and giggling, and the little kids are throwing things at each other," said Jeremy Finn, one of the authors of an article published by the *Review of Educational Research*. "But in a small class, the first thing a teacher says is 'Let's all bring our chairs around me here in a circle.' "

Students in smaller classes also describe themselves as having better relationships with their teachers, and they evaluate both their classes and their teachers more positively than do their peers in larger classes, according to the National Council of Teachers of English.

The United States had made progress on this front, but reducing class size is expensive. This option says we need to spend what it takes to shrink class sizes.

Cancel student loan debt if students complete a year of national service in underserved communities.

Many young people are dropping out of college because of the student debt crisis. The Pew Research Center found that, for the first time in more than 130 years, Americans ages 18-34 are more likely to be living with their parents than independently with a spouse or partner, partly because of rising student loan debt.

In 2020, 45 million students owed a total of $1.6 trillion, making student loan debt the second highest consumer debt category—trailing only mortgage loan debt and higher than both credit card and auto loan debt. In 2019, the Federal Reserve reported that over 1 in 7 student loan borrowers were more than 90 days delinquent on their payments. This kind of debt hinders a borrower's ability to buy a home, start a business, and save for retirement.

Black and Latinx students are at a particular disadvantage, a 2019 report from the Center for Responsible Lending noted. Systemic racism and discriminatory practices have left Black and Latinx individuals with less familial wealth and higher levels of debt. Furthermore, the gender wage gap makes it harder for young women to repay their student

loans. The American Association of University Women found in 2020 that women tend to owe more than their male counterparts, while Black women and Latinas are burdened by the highest debt of all.

Student loan forgiveness coupled with a requirement for national service can ensure that more young people enter the workforce debt free while, at the same time, helping communities address critical needs.

Greatly expand mentorship and internship programs that expose young people to the work skills that jobs require or encourage them to complete their schooling.

Young people improve their chances for being successful when they surround themselves with people who offer encouragement and help in starting their careers. A study of Big Brothers Big Sisters programs across the country found that students who meet regularly with their mentors are 52 percent less likely than their peers to skip a day of school and 37 percent less likely to skip a class.

There are over 46 million young people, ages 8-18, in the United States, and 16 million of them never interact with a mentor. One out of every three young people does not have an adult outside the family home who can be trusted for advice and guidance. Through mentorship and internship programs, young people build confidence as they gain experience, knowledge, and skills.

Increase mental health and well-being services to improve the quality of life for all ages.

Three out of four people with mental health problems show signs of their illness before the age of 24, according to the US Department of Health and Human Services. There are growing concerns that if we do not adequately fund mental

health care for all Americans, but especially for young people, communities and the nation will pay the price later.

The Johns Hopkins University Bloomberg School of Public Health reports that mental illness accounts for more than $200 billion of the nation's $3 trillion annual health-care spending, but that investment often falls short of what's needed. The cuts to many state mental health budgets, which worsened during the coronavirus pandemic, have created a public health emergency in which people with serious mental illness such as schizophrenia and bipolar disorder get inadequate treatment and end up homeless or in prison—or worse.

In November 2013, Virginia state Senator Creigh Deeds' 24-year-old son, Gus, was evaluated by mental health professionals who were forced to release him because there were no psychiatric beds available in hospitals where he could receive the necessary treatment. At home, less than 24 hours later, Gus stabbed his father in the chest and head multiple times and then committed suicide. Senator Deeds, who survived the attack, told "60 Minutes" that more could have been done. "The system failed my son," he said.

Trade-Offs and Downsides

■ Reducing class sizes and providing extra support to students will cost more money, which likely would be obtained by raising property taxes.

■ Trading student debt forgiveness for national service means needy students do service work while those whose families can afford to pay for college can get on with their lives and careers.

■ Companies and communities rarely design high-quality mentorship programs, and internships often pay little or no money.

■ Creating more mental health programs will cost money and may hinder young people from becoming resilient and self-sufficient. We should not medicalize every problem.

Questions for deliberation . . .

1 Reducing class sizes, forgiving college debt, and expanding mentoring and mental health services will not be free. Where should the money come from? In your own community, what kinds of tax increases or cuts in services would you support in order to pay for these proposals?

2 Are large class sizes and lack of extra support the most crucial problems in education? What about improving teacher training or efforts to retain good teachers in substandard schools or raising standards? If we could make only one or two changes in education, what should they be?

3 Is eliminating student loan debt fair to students and families who save for college or to students who work their way through college, choose to go part time, or choose less expensive schools in order to keep their debt to a minimum?

Option 2:
Give Everyone a Fair Chance

IN ORDER TO CREATE A SOCIETY in which everyone has a fair chance of succeeding, regardless of race or class, we need to dismantle systemic barriers to education, earnings, and equality. Long-standing economic and social obstacles have for too long denied opportunities to women and to millions of Americans from diverse racial and ethnic backgrounds.

The US Census Bureau predicts that, by 2050, non-White racial and ethnic groups will constitute a majority of the population. Yet these demographic shifts are not leading to improved outcomes for many Americans. Income inequality is on the rise, and the gender pay gap still exists, both of which disproportionately affect people of color.

In this view, the United States will continue to be an uneven playing field until we make progress toward rectifying the unequal distribution of income and wealth. According to the Pew Research Center, from 2007 to 2016, the median net worth of the top 20 percent increased 13 percent, to $1.2 million.

Meanwhile, families who earned an average of $32,100 in 2007 saw their incomes fall to $19,500 in 2016. And although US household wealth rose slightly before the COVID-19 pandemic, 2020 data from the Federal Reserve show that inequality persists, and there are growing concerns that inequities could deepen as some workers lose their jobs and incomes due to pandemic-related shutdowns.

Research consistently shows distinct patterns of inequality in terms of income and wealth among American families. The Pew Research Center found that, based on census data, the median White household income in 2018 was $84,600, while that of Black households was $51,600. This gap has remained for decades. Looking at overall wealth, the disparity is even more stark. According to the Federal Reserve, the 2019 median household wealth of White families was $188,200. For Hispanic families, the number was $36,100, while for Black families it was just $24,100.

Gender disparities in wages are another indicator of pervasive inequalities. In 2019, women made 85 cents to every dollar made by a man in a similar job and women were more likely than men to be among the working poor.

This option says that we must develop public policies that promote inclusion and safeguard people from discrimination as well as take practical steps, such as raising the minimum wage and providing free community college, to give all young people in our country a chance at a fair start—now and in the future.

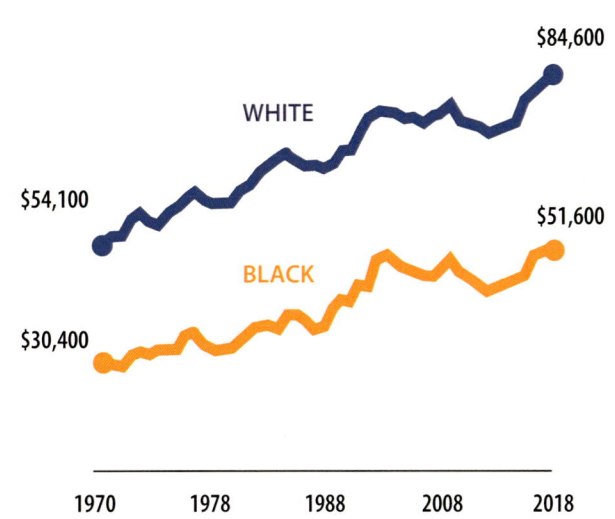

Black-White Income Gap since 1970

Median US Household Income, in 2018 Dollars

NOTE: Income is adjusted for household size and scaled to reflect a three-person household.

SOURCE: Pew Research Center analysis of 1970 to 2019 Current Population Survey, Annual Social and Economic Supplements

A Primary Drawback of This Option:

Public policies that mandate equitable treatment cannot eradicate bias or change the hearts and minds of citizens. Creating a fairer society is a slow process that may not have immediate benefits. Affirmative action policies, intended to help level the playing field, have often been seen as "reverse racism" that limits opportunities for White Americans.

What We Should Do

Increase the minimum wage to improve household incomes and reduce childhood poverty.

The federal minimum wage has been $7.25 an hour for most workers since July 2009. That is not a living wage for a family. Though many states and localities have set their minimum wage above that level, we need to increase the federal minimum wage to boost incomes across the board. This would go a long way toward giving young people from lower-income families a fair shot at fulfilling their potential.

Increasing the minimum wage also would help reduce race-based and gender-based economic disparities. For instance, in 2018 there was a 25 percent gap between the average annual earnings of Black and White workers, and in 2019 the gender wage gap continued.

Few things other than raising the minimum wage would have such an immediate impact for young workers. In 2019, 1.2 million workers ages 16-34 earned wages at or below $7.25 an hour.

Eliminate standardized testing and assess students through teacher evaluations of student achievement and behavior.

Standardized testing is an artificial and, at times, biased barrier that holds some young people back from realizing their full potential. People should be able to continue their education or take advantage of new opportunities without being unfairly held back by low test scores. Many Americans worry that standardized testing tends to measure performance more than knowledge, asking students to simply recite information they have memorized.

Researchers have noted a history of racial, cultural, and socioeconomic bias in standardized testing. Specifically, in 2017, experts at the Brookings Institution analyzed racial differences in the math section of the general SAT test, using College Board population data for the nearly 1.7 million college-bound seniors. They found that the SAT questions and scoring methods reflect and reinforce racial disparities.

Studies have shown that the designers of standardized tests regularly rely on questions that assume background knowledge more often held by White, middle-class students than by many minority students. Psychologists have even expressed concerns that Black and Hispanic students often confront negative stereotypes about their testing performance, which causes undue stress and anxiety that can ultimately lead to lower test scores.

Teachers say standardized tests do not provide an accurate assessment of what has been learned and that it cannot be determined from answers on such tests whether students could apply that learning to real-world situations outside the classroom. The exams are often criticized for creating a climate in which teachers feel pressured to "teach to the test" so struggling students can pass state assessments and other exams.

Constantine Pankin/Shutterstock.com

Make community college free and guarantee that students who graduate can then enter four-year colleges.

In the last decade, the average tuition and fees at private four-year colleges and universities rose 26 percent, and they climbed 35 percent at four-year public institutions.

Although not every American will go to college, there are distinct benefits to continuing one's education. Colleges prepare young people intellectually and socially for careers and adulthood. Getting a college degree usually leads to better paying and more highly skilled jobs with benefits that include health-care coverage, retirement plans, paid time off, flexible schedules, and other perks.

Yet the rising cost of college has put these lifelong advantages beyond the reach of many, especially low-income families. Bringing college within reach for more young people would be a significant boost to their futures.

One solution may be the nation's community college system. Community colleges, sometimes unfairly seen as inferior to four-year universities, could be an effective way to get more Americans educated and employed in a shorter period of time.

Community college is significantly less expensive than a four-year school. According to the College Board, in the 2019-2020 school year, the average published tuition and fees were $3,730 at two-year public colleges, compared to $10,440 at in-state four-year public colleges and universities and $36,880 at four-year private colleges and universities.

However, getting from community college into a four-year institution is not easy. According to the National Student Clearinghouse Research Center, only 30 percent of community college students succeeded in transferring to a four-year institution in 2017. Community college students usually find it difficult to transfer their completed course credits so, if and when they gain acceptance to a four-year school, they end up taking out more loans and spending

more money to cover the costs of courses similar to ones they already completed.

Make K-12 US history curricula more inclusive by acknowledging the contributions and experiences of immigrants and enslaved and indigenous peoples.

School boards and state education departments need to reexamine how schools teach students about the roles and experiences of immigrants and enslaved and indigenous peoples in US history to provide a more accurate account of and a deeper appreciation for the contributions made by them and their descendants.

Differing perspectives matter. A 2010 study from Harvard University found that students' self-esteem improves when they regularly encounter positive depictions of people who look like them. Ninth- and 10th-grade female students performed significantly better on a chemistry quiz when the textbook lessons featured images of only female scientists, while the performance of boys declined under the same conditions.

"If we had a better understanding of other people's experience with things such as immigration or activities such as removing people—the impact that they have—I think then we would be less susceptible to inaccurate narratives and more capable of responding in thoughtful ways," wrote Edwin Schupman in *Smithsonian* magazine. Schupman, a citizen of the Muscogee (Creek) Nation, is manager of Native Knowledge 360 Degrees, an educational initiative aimed at improving the way in which Native American history and culture is taught in US schools.

Forty-eight percent of young Americans ages 6-21 are members of non-White racial and ethnic groups, according to a 2018 report from the Pew Research Center. School lesson plans should tap into that diversity by making sure the retelling of historic events includes multiple accounts and perspectives from verified sources.

Trade-Offs and Downsides

■ Increasing the minimum wage may put some small companies out of business, reducing jobs rather than encouraging job growth. Wage hikes are not an automatic cure for poverty in the United States.

■ Standardized tests give essential information about students' reading, math, and reasoning levels. We must have an impartial metric that assesses student learning and performance to complement subjective assessments by teachers who may have many different standards or have been known to show bias or favoritism to certain students.

■ Hundreds of thousands of young people have worked to earn scholarships, saved money from high-school jobs, and worked their way through college to emerge stronger and better prepared for life in the real world. There are more urgent needs for tax dollars than financing two-year colleges.

■ This is potentially a massive overhaul of the curriculum, which will require extensive retraining, and there is no way to ensure teachers will comply with mandated changes to curricula or create inclusive learning environments for all students.

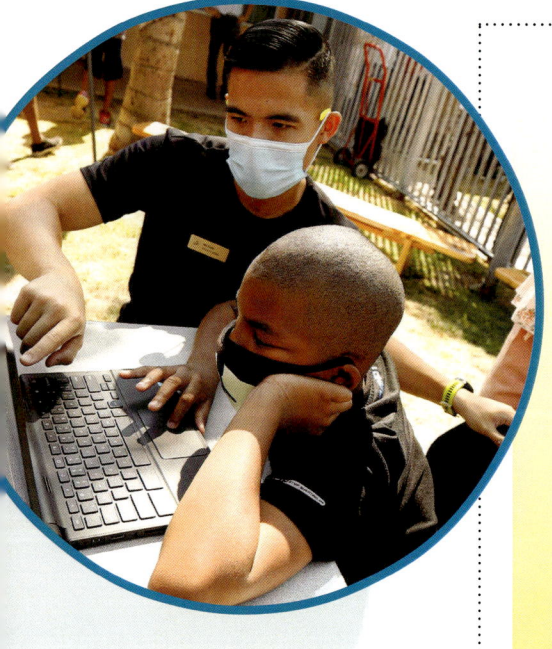

Questions for deliberation . . .

1 This option explores actions aimed at creating a more equitable society for all Americans. Can legislation and other policy changes really reduce bias? If not, what would?

2 How far would raising the minimum wage go in reducing child poverty? Is it a major step forward or only a minor one? What other changes might be more important?

3 If we eliminate standardized tests in K-12 schools, should we eliminate them in licensing for professionals such as doctors, lawyers, and accountants? Do standardized tests have any benefits in our society?

Option 3:
Focus on Economic Security

AFTER DECADES OF BORROWING by the federal government, the next generation is inheriting a "fixer upper," a house in need of much repair. Our rising national debt has put our country on an unstable footing, limiting our ability to invest in future growth or to prepare for crises. The United States is on an unsustainable path, and it is long past time to make the necessary reforms to secure our fiscal future.

The need for immediate and direct action is urgent: the US Census Bureau projects that by 2050, Americans ages 65 and older will likely outnumber those younger than 18. As the population of retirees—and beneficiaries of Social Security and Medicare—grows faster than the population of workers, expenses for safety net programs will grow faster than income, a shift that will put an even greater strain on the finances of these programs.

These are not remote concerns for today's young people. A ballooning national debt, crumbling infrastructure, the national failure to embrace renewable energy, and the threat of climate

change all have real impacts on the young people of today and tomorrow. Even the viability of Social Security is not a question for just older generations; more than 1 in 4 of today's 20-year-olds will likely receive Social Security disability benefits before retirement age, according to the Social Security Administration.

"More debt and higher deficits not only harm the economy, they dip into the pocketbooks of average Americans," said Maya MacGuineas, of the nonpartisan Committee for a Responsible Federal Budget, in an interview with *USA TODAY*. Debt and deficit increases drive up interest rates, which slows economic growth. "Slower growth leads to lower wages," MacGuineas points out.

Younger generations are already seeing less federal investment in their futures than ever before, and the rising national debt means that interest is crowding out the government's ability to invest in programs such as education, infrastructure, and research and development. Most Americans believe that in the next 30 years, the nation will have a

weaker economy, a growing income divide, a broken political system, and a degraded environment, according to a 2019 study by the Pew Research Center.

This option says we need to take steps at every level to address the problems that threaten to bankrupt or weaken the nation. Americans should change their habits and expectations, communities should find local solutions to persistent problems, we should reduce our reliance on fossil fuels, and legislators should reform long-standing federal programs to ensure that future generations inherit an economically and environmentally sound country.

A Primary Drawback of This Option:

Partisan gridlock often hinders efforts to craft and enact legislation that addresses perennial problems. By the time these issues are attended to, today's youth could have reached retirement age.

What We Should Do

Fully fund all new federal programs either through higher taxes, spending, or a combination of both.

When policymakers spend money we don't have on programs and services without making meaningful reforms, our children and grandchildren are the ones who ultimately pay the price. The next generations deserve a future free of crippling debt.

The federal deficit, caused by the government spending more than the revenues it brings in, grew rapidly in 2020, largely due to federal funds spent on mitigating the economic damage of the coronavirus pandemic. However, the deficit was large and growing before the onset of the pandemic, and it is disrupting the nation's ability to address long-term fiscal challenges. It also means that the federal government must borrow even more money to cover its commitments. By the fall of 2020, the national debt, the total amount owed after years of deficits, stood at $21 trillion. Foreign investors hold over one-third of US debt.

A national debt of this size will not go away overnight, and reducing it will require the political will to make difficult and painful choices. But the alternative, an ever-larger drag on the nation's economic engine, is even worse. According to this option, we need to begin taking action now. At the same time, lawmakers need to boost the prospects of Social Security and Medicare, which face long-term financing shortfalls under currently scheduled benefits and financing. Both programs are experiencing cost growth substantially in excess of GDP growth because of a growing older population that is living longer and facing increasing health-care costs.

Local utilities should invest in switching to renewable energy sources to combat climate change and create opportunities for clean jobs.

The use of renewable energy resources is on the rise. In 2019, consumption of biofuels, geothermal, solar, and wind energy in the United States was nearly three times greater than in 2000. About 17 percent of total US electricity generation was from renewable energy sources. We can and should use more renewable energy.

In September 2019, hundreds of thousands of young Americans, along with millions of young people from other countries, participated in coordinated protests that demanded urgent action on climate change.

Investing in renewables also has vast economic benefits that can help employ and sustain the next generation. Through the creation of clean "green" jobs, states, cities, and businesses can put young people to work in careers that improve the efficiency of energy, bring down emissions of greenhouse gases, minimize all forms of waste and pollution, and protect or restore ecosystems. Finally, investing in renewables has the potential for ensuring that this nation will, once and for all, become energy independent.

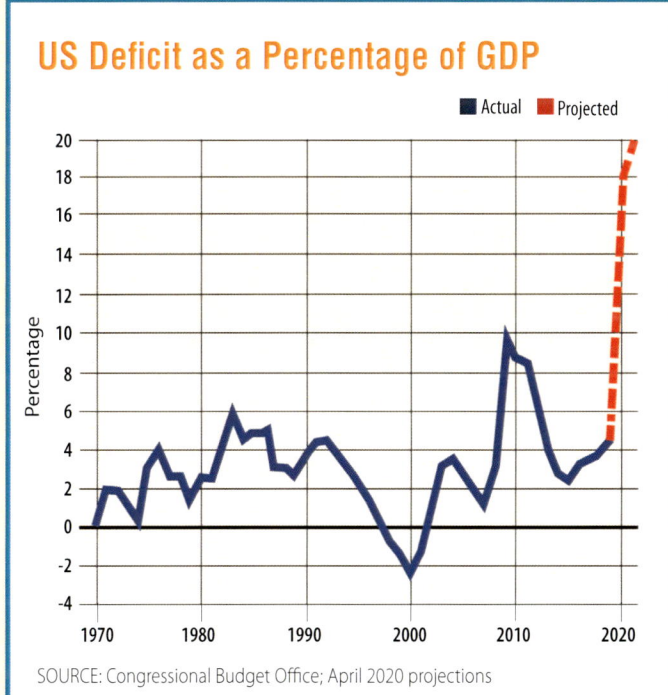

US Deficit as a Percentage of GDP

Legend: ■ Actual ■ Projected

y-axis: Percentage (−4 to 20)
x-axis: 1970, 1980, 1990, 2000, 2010, 2020

SOURCE: Congressional Budget Office; April 2020 projections

Invest in building and repairing deteriorating roads and bridges and in other infrastructure projects.

Decades of neglect to our infrastructure mean communities across the country now have dangerously crumbling bridges, roads, and highways in serious need of repair; outdated and energy-inefficient buildings; and inadequate public transport, among other critical needs. This weakens the economy and hands off yet another responsibility to future generations.

In its latest report card on the condition of US infrastructure in 2017, the American Society of Civil Engineers gave our infrastructure a D+ or "poor" rating. The group estimated it would cost $4.6 trillion to bring the country's infrastructure into a state of repair that would earn it a grade of B by 2025. But only about 55 percent of the necessary funds have been committed to key projects. Improving roads and bridges alone would require $1.1 trillion more than states, localities, and the federal government have allocated. The economic impact caused by the coronavirus pandemic and the legislative response to it is likely to sideline those efforts.

Investing in infrastructure can stabilize the economy and provide millions of jobs each year in construction and maintenance. A Brookings Institution analysis of federal data showed 14 million people have jobs in fields directly related to infrastructure. From engineers to electrical power line installers and construction workers, people working on infrastructure account for nearly 11 percent of the nation's workforce.

Cities and counties, as well as consumers, should do business only with companies that hire more American workers and open new factories in the United States. It's time to end the outsourcing of jobs and production to foreign countries.

Outsourcing American jobs to foreign countries is a concerning trend that must be addressed in order to create a stable economic environment for future generations. Too many products from American manufacturers are actually made in factories overseas.

The General Motors (GM) Transmission Operations plant in Warren, Michigan, was one of five GM factories closed in North America by the end of 2019. The closings displaced hundreds of workers and created economic hardship across the state. University of Michigan economists estimated that the plant closings could mean 16,000 fewer jobs in Michigan between 2020 and 2022.

Since 2000, the United States has lost over five million manufacturing jobs. Manufacturing plants also declined sharply between 1998 and 2008, shrinking by more than 51,000 sites.

Experts from the Economic Policy Institute report that jobs outsourced to China have hurt American job opportunities and have contributed to wage erosion since 2001, when China entered the World Trade Organization. Between 2001 and 2018, the growing trade deficit with China cost the US 3.7 million jobs, and three quarters of those jobs were in manufacturing. Today, in 2020, this deficit is higher than ever.

This is not a matter for just federal officials to grapple with. States, communities, and individuals should focus on buying local and supporting American-made products to give manufacturers an incentive to keep jobs in the United States.

Trade-Offs and Downsides

■ Ensuring all government programs are paid without deficit funding would require cutting essential programs or raising taxes or both, which would stunt growth. Such a strategy could also result in gridlock about which programs to cut and taxes to expand.

■ Switching to renewable energy likely will require large up-front capital investments that utilities would pass on to consumers through higher user rates.

■ Building and repairing deteriorating roads and bridges and other infrastructure projects are major undertakings that would add to our national debt, require higher taxes to fund, or divert funds from other critical programs.

■ Ending or reducing overseas production and the outsourcing of jobs will likely increase prices for US consumers for many products.

Questions for deliberation . . .

1 States and communities nationwide are suffering from the pandemic and the economic downturn it has brought. Is it realistic to end deficit spending now?

2 The country was running deficits even when the economy was thriving because raising taxes, cutting spending, or doing both upsets voters. What specific spending would you be willing to cut? Would you be willing to cut any spending that you typically support?

3 Is it possible or even wise to try to keep all American factories open and protect all American manufacturing jobs? Could this have unintended consequences? What might go wrong if we pursued this policy fully?

4 Whose jobs will be replaced or displaced by the transition to renewable energy sources, and how should we retrain them?

Closing Reflections

THINKING THROUGH KEY IDEAS and acting on specific proposals presented in this issue guide will bring about changes that affect Americans of every age, gender, race, and socioeconomic background.

Succeeding generations should inherit a society that is fairer and fiscally sound. Before ending the forum, take some time to revisit some of the central questions this guide raises:

- What should be done to make sure young people can live up to their potential?
- We can't do everything, so what matters most to us?
- Since all our choices have trade-offs, what kinds of decisions and actions are most likely to provide succeeding generations a prosperous future?
- What are the risks of the ideas we tend to support? Could some of them have unintended consequences?
- Are there perspectives in the ideas we oppose that we need to seriously consider?
- When we make choices in our communities and at the ballot box, how will our decisions affect others in different circumstances?
- Should the needs and expectations of future generations take priority over our current needs?
- What do younger and older generations owe each other? What responsibilities do younger Americans have for older people, particularly those who are in ill health or struggling to make ends meet?

Other important questions to consider are these: On what do we agree? About what do we need to talk more? From whom else should we hear? What else do we need to know? How do the ideas and options in this guide affect what we do as individuals or as members of a community? How might our actions affect the nation and the future?

Summary

Option 1:
Equip People to Succeed

MANY YOUNG PEOPLE NEED MORE EDUCATION AND TRAINING TO REALIZE THEIR FULL POTENTIAL AND LEAD SUCCESSFUL LIVES. This option says that we must rethink what it means to prepare young people for a vastly different social and economic landscape through the rest of this century. The global economy is fueling competition, while automation is shrinking the number of jobs. A greater share of the jobs that remain will require a college degree or other advanced training.

A Primary Drawback
This does too little to teach self-reliance, personal responsibility, or a good work ethic and assumes that all challenges can be overcome with more services. But even the best preparation doesn't ensure success in life. There are many forces that determine our individual and collective futures.

ACTIONS	DRAWBACKS
Boost K-12 student achievement by reducing class sizes and providing extra support to students who need it.	This would require more teachers and increases in school district budgets and property taxes.
Allow students to have student loan debt canceled if they complete a year of national service in underserved communities.	More affluent young people will bypass national service while middle and working class students lose a year in the pursuit of their career goals.
Greatly expand mentorship and internship programs where engaged adults will expose young people to the work skills that jobs require or encourage them to complete their schooling.	Companies rarely design high-quality internship programs, and internships, which often pay little or nothing, typically go to children of privileged families who can afford them.
Increase services and resources for mental health and well-being to increase chances that young people can take advantage of their opportunities.	If we medicalize every problem, we won't be teaching young people about how to be resilient and self-sufficient.
What else could we do?	What's the trade-off if we do that?

Summary

Option 2:

Give Everyone a Fair Chance

NOT EVERYONE IN THE UNITED STATES HAS AN EQUAL CHANCE TO SUCCEED.
Entrenched biases toward race, religion, gender identity, and sexual orientation have created an uneven playing field. This not only unjustly creates serious barriers for millions of young people but also deprives society of the contributions many of them would have made if they had access to the same opportunities enjoyed by their more fortunate peers. This option says that if we want to harness the potential of the next generation's creativity and diversity, we need to safeguard people against unfair treatment.

A Primary Drawback
Even policies that mandate equitable treatment cannot eradicate bias or change the hearts and minds of citizens. Affirmative action policies, intended to help level the playing field, have often been seen as "reverse racism" that limits opportunities for White Americans.

ACTIONS	DRAWBACKS
Increase the minimum wage to improve household incomes and reduce child poverty.	This will put some small companies out of business, reducing jobs rather than increasing them.
Eliminate standardized testing, which disadvantages minority students, and instead, assess students through teacher evaluations.	Standardized tests give essential information about students' reading, math, and knowledge levels. Individual teachers may have low standards or favor students they like.
Make community college free, and guarantee that students could then enter four-year colleges.	Not everyone who completes community college is ready for a four-year institution. This will make some colleges less selective.
Make K-12 US history curricula more inclusive by acknowledging the contributions and experiences of slaves, immigrants, and indigenous peoples.	This will require lots of retraining and will be a major change, possibly at the expense of important American concepts. History teachers can barely get through the basics as it is.
What else could we do?	What's the trade-off if we do that?

Summary

Option 3:

Focus on Economic Security

DEEP-ROOTED PROBLEMS IN OUR SOCIETY HAVE NOT BEEN ADDRESSED, PUTTING THE NEXT GENERATION AT RISK. Our rising national debt has put our country on an unstable footing, limiting our ability to invest in future growth or tackle present challenges. This option holds that we cannot make progress on other fronts if we don't address the problems that threaten to bankrupt us. We need to increase and sustain our efforts to leave a more secure economy for future generations.

A Primary Drawback

Partisan gridlock often hinders efforts to craft and pass legislation that addresses perennial problems. By the time these issues are attended to, today's youth will be retirement age.

ACTIONS	DRAWBACKS
End deficit spending and begin containing the federal debt.	This would require across-the-board cuts in needed programs and force tax hikes that will extend the current economic recession rather than shorten it.
Local utilities should invest in switching to renewable energy sources to combat climate change and create opportunities for clean jobs.	Utilities will likely have to raise consumers' rates, which hurts low-income families and small businesses.
Invest in building and repairing roads, bridges, and other infrastructure.	Major investments like this would add to our national debt, require higher taxes to fund projects, or divert funds from other needed programs.
Cities and counties, as well as consumers, should do business only with companies that hire American workers and build factories in the US. It's time to end the outsourcing of jobs and production to foreign countries.	This will increase prices on food and consumer goods, limit buyers' choices, and could lead to shortages and less international trade.
What else could we do?	**What's the trade-off if we do that?**

The National Issues Forums

The National Issues Forums (NIF) is a network of organizations that bring together citizens around the nation to talk about pressing social and political issues of the day. Thousands of community organizations—including schools, libraries, churches, civic groups, and others—have held forums designed to give people a public voice in the affairs of their communities and their nation.

Forum participants engage in deliberation, which is simply weighing options for action against things held commonly valuable. This calls upon them to listen respectfully to others, sort out their views in terms of what they most value, consider courses of action and their disadvantages, and seek to identify areas of common ground for action.

Issue guides like this one are designed to support these conversations. They present varying perspectives on the issue at hand, suggest actions to address identified problems, and note the trade-offs of taking those actions to remind participants that all solutions have costs as well as benefits.

In this way, forum participants move from holding individual opinions to making collective choices as members of a community—the kinds of choices from which public policy may be forged or collective action may be taken at community as well as national levels.

Forum Questionnaire

If you participated in this forum, please fill out a questionnaire, which is included in this issue guide or can be accessed online at **www.nifi.org/questionnaires**. If you are filling out the enclosed questionnaire, please return the completed form to your moderator or to the National Issues Forums Institute, 100 Commons Road, Dayton, Ohio 45459.

If you moderated this forum, please fill out a Moderator Response sheet, which is online at **www.nifi.org/questionnaires**.